Ripples

on the

Pond

© Steve Wilkinson 2015

All rights reserved

No part of this book may be copied by mechanical or electronic means without the prior consent of the copyright holder.

Published through The Bamboo Hut Press

## Introduction

Poetry surrounds us. The wind blowing though the trees, the sea tide gently rising and falling, birdsong from the undergrowth, all speak to the poets ear. Nature is a great inspirer.

At times it may be the complexities of human relationships that give birth to poems.

Love, seperation, death and grief supply an endless array of topics that manifest themselves as poems.

In this collection of tanshi or short poems I have included the above subjects, some are obvious, others are more subtle.

Many are haiku or haiku-like in nature, some are written in five lines as tanka or gogyoshi.

I have deliberately avoided setting the poems out in any kind of subject order so that the reader may dip in and out of the book at random and hopefully discover something new each time.

Please enjoy this tanshi collection of "Ripples on the Pond"

Steve Wilkinson

Ripples on the Pond

sunny day -
even the sparrows
look colourful


wagtails
flying
over the reservoir
I feel the valley breeze
and think of you


day by day
the cherries on the tree
change from green to red -
the warning signs
were always there

Spring tide -
how gently the moon
rises and falls


Saturday night
two teenagers
huddled in a doorway
share a kiss ...
a promise


June evening -
taking nearly an hour
to say goodnight

nothing left to say or do -
the cawing of crows




twigs and leaves
on the park bench -
heavy rain




How often
we spoke of leaving and now
this endless rain




billions spent on armaments -
on a street in Rio
a childs empty bowl

at the feeder
the mother blue tit
feeds her young -
I read in the news
about more child abuse




coming and going
coming and going all day -
birds on the feeder




boiling rice -
outside the rain falls faster




summer heat -
a cloud passes
from one pane to another

tyre tracks
through an open field
all the times
we spoke about leaving
and yet.....




tell me your name
before you breathe your last
 I need to remember
 as I slip from this world
 that I touched someones soul




Normandy
the summer of 44
thousands
lie motionless
on a bloody beach

the quiet coldness
of the night air after rain
now
the argument is over
the atmosphere begins to cool


late evening -
a song thrush serenades the moon


a pebble
thrown into the pond-
ripples
travel towards me
as you turn and walk away

morning rain
a dark cloud
covers the heart
bringing silence
to the young birds song


dawn chorus -
another song
I never learned to sing


Virtual flowers -
you tell me you're sorry
in a text message


summer night -
the wood carver throws a log into his fire drum

gentle evening rain -
the warbling song of an unknown bird


putting down thoughts
in an empty book
is the way it always was
the encouragement I craved
was spelt c.o.n.t.e.m.p.t


the silence between us
when will it break ?
It is not silence
but the sound
of two hearts teetering

after the rain -
the smell of the earth


thunder clouds -
a frightened child
hides from its mother


wild mallow scent -
a wood pigeon
balances on a soaked branch


sudden shower -
a rush of air
through the open window

spelling out the future
with charts and graphs and words
and still this anguish



the speaker spoke about Lazarus
 through the open window
the entrancing song of the song thrush



wedding anniversary DVD night -
"12 years a slave "

coming together
somewhere distant
old railway tracks -
I think my great great granddad
hammered this one into place



standing here
feeling the sea breeze
clothe me
the tang of salt spray
and I'm ten once more



Crashing waves
pounding the pier around midday -
lies
rolled off your tongue
as easily as the tide

pouring
out my heart into a glass
marked tomorrow
yesterday has drained the bottle
leaving only the dregs



bowing their heads
the peonies after the rain -
we stood
around the grave
looking into ourselves



deep into night
the sound of owls
penetrates -
alone in the kitchen
one cup one saucer

another dull day
grey,overcast,damp
down the street
workmen on a rooftop
installing solar panels



finding solace
in the written words
of dead poets
speaking to my heart
so locked into the past



left alone
to live out her days
in a chair
overlooking the park
was I really young once ?

stepping out
into a future
I make with words
watching rain fall
on forgotten streets



a creaking start
to another day
oiling the joints and the mind
with the solace
of unconditional surrender



standing here
watching the river
bend out of sight -
the hidden feeling
of not knowing what I did wrong

still affected
by your departure
so long ago -
seasons of wilderness life
still keep me guessing




the blueness
of the autumn sky -
in the cemetery
the smell of pine needles
crushed under my feet




20 years
walking the beat
in a tough town -
he thought he knew what fear was
until the doctor said cancer

barely brushing
the rhododendrons...
summer sunset
too many promises
lost in the windfall


in the distance
where the street lights end-
a new leaf


frost on the grass
of a spring morning..
despite my reflection I feel young within


temple bell..
from across the river geese take flight

Lying awake
listening to the sound
of summer rain -
filled with uncertainty
I replay the scene again and again




standing naked in the rain-
autumn willow



following  dreams-
I watch a seagull become a speck



removing your gown -
a white chrysanthemum

writing her name on my hand-
first crush

in a hovel or in a palace-
the full moon

in his basket
groceries for one
I reach out
and take hold
of my wifes hand

scentless flowers -
and now the evening rain

a curlew skims across the heather -
twilight



the memories
of that hot summer night called to her
" mama I'm thirsty "



at eighteen
they held a garden party
just for her -
despite the August sun
she still wore long sleeves



a green moon appears as the bottle empties -
summer evening

my dreams -
flower petals rise and fall
on the rippling pond




dry grass shivering in the breeze-
I cast petals into the sky
and wish you my blessing




dark hills
blue sky white clouds -
all the colours of my solitude

quivering grass
and the scent of jasmine
all to quickly
my sun has set
on your memory




at your touch
my face
becomes the sun
shining on maple leaves




hot date -
I convinced myself she would wear red

summer rain -
the dead bird in the garden
stares at the sky


smooth jazz -
all the walls are painted blue


a la carte menu -
I wonder if she'll say yes


summer rain -
I feel my blood sugar plummet

morning stillness -
between here and there
a shadow


the report said
she went to rehab -
as if that
made any difference
when they lowered her coffin


sudden downpour-
at a window by the river
a face

after school
school boys climbing
on garden walls
as for me
I was always afraid
of taking the next step



In the waiting room
a mother
making strange faces at her baby -
I was always so concerned
how I appeared to others



after the thunderstorm-
forgiveness

so many ways
to say I am sorry -
a gift of purple hyacinths


spilling five lines
and then deleting them
for another time
I drink what remains
and call it tanka


across the remains of a fossilized tree -
slow growing ivy

Washing
blowing in the wind -
you always allowed
others
to make the choices




Listening
to the birds singing
insects buzzing
I watch the pulse in my wrist,
drink coffee and wait




so short a time
to sample this life -
your tiny coffin
consumed
by flowers

watching you walk out of my life
in the distance
the 8;42 trundles by



Not certain
where this road will lead -
the practise
of taking wrong turns
lead me to you



another
t.v. dinner for one
one year older
I am now the box
that the present came in

If you see her
walking beneath red street lights
tell her
I still remember her
and the way she used to smile




contemplating -
I wear my imperfections
like a Sunday suit
needing a redeemer
to iron out the creases




Trying to define tanka -
I ask friends just how many colours
are in the sunset

looking
in the shop window
does she admire that expensive dress
or maybe her own reflection ?


the pitter patter sound on my windowsill
morning rain
and the promise of peace


summer sunset -
the goalkeeper shields his eyes


World cup stadia -
on the streets of Brazil
a child of ten summers begs for money

how many ways
to describe this weight
an anchor
or a millstone
tied to the jagged edges of my heart




There is no need
to tell me its raining -
I have felt the rain fall all of my life




looking back
I can see where the paths bent out of sight
we walked blindly you and I in and out of love

another death
sensationalized
but out there
this was someones child
someones heart and breath



the almost silent sound
of reminiscence
taps on my shoulder
how many times must I quieten
the anguish that calls



above fields of ripening barley -
skylarks song

dog rose scent -
drowned by the constant flow
of morning traffic




beneath the lime tree
yellow lichen
clings to an old wooden fence




its not the burden thats tired me out
only the length of time I've had to carry it




Just evading the lawnmowers blades
a butterfly takes flight -
I read the doctors letter one more time

hot night -
the smell of summer through an open window


This life so full of pain -
on our journey tonight we meet briefly in
dreams


until we split
we shared nothing in common
now at least
we are able to share
our mutually assured hatred


Constantly looking
for our place in this crazy world
only to find it right beneath our feet

and so it ended
with nothing more than a smile
but behind her eyes
I sensed a message
I would never hear



All the parts of my life
run in converging lines
all beyond     my reach
outside my   control



Normal people do they really exist?
I count my fingers expecting to find an airtight answer

your eyes as you were leaving -
birdsong



growing older -
the tree outside my window and me



Oh yes
I almost forgot
we don't love each other anymore -
old habits are hard to break



Red maple leaves
strewn across the bridge
the white one
where once
we walked

Alone
in the candlelight
memories
poured from the wine bottle
intensify with each sip



Lengthening shadows -
on this spring evening
we talk about past times
reminiscing
over sweet tea



Harsh sunlight
on the concrete road -
times passage
does nothing
to soften the longing

rising from the dust
the child
baptized in the dirt
hopes
he will not spend his life there


I stare at the photograph
so long ago
before the pain
etched lines
in your beauty


A heap
of snow covered rags
beneath them
someone
stirs

We picked flowers
in the long grass of the meadow
we lay down
the sun shining from our eyes
in an ecstasy born from love




I searched the depths
of that innermost part of you
we clung to each other
believing that love would always
light the fire to make us burn




half moon -
reminding me
that without you
I am less
than whole

Cascading snow
sliding from rooftops
beneath the eaves -
a cat is listening
to the song of a robin



Rewriting
old poems -
trying
once again
to find myself



Still searching -
he kneels
before the altar
a bleeding heart
imploring bleeding hands

I buried the past
in a simple grave -
no epitaph
just a stone
saying "I was here"



the constant flow
of car after car after car
through the town -
so many hearts
heading for a heart attack



philosophy students
in the city
heading for the pub

a happy life
how much is needed ?
how much is not ?


standing firm
even this windstorm is powerless -
I adjust my sails and carry on regardless


I sought perfection
in the imperfect world
I found truth
in the flaws of others

at the foot
of the mountain -
my foot


storm clouds
on the horizon-
I open your letter


Sabbath day-
in the garden
the buzzing of bees


distant thunder-
you tell me
about the affair

lightening strike-
the penny
finally drops


winter rain-
suitcases standing
in the fading light


spring thaw-
never enough time
to say I'm sorry


old photograph-
the rose bushes
first buds

high noon-
the shadow
returns to the tree



autumn rain
falling on my nostalgia -
nothing remains
of the place we once
held close to our hearts



after years
of wondering -
the first handful
of soil
answers all my questions

he lived alone
never once
did they hear him cry -
the widower
after twenty years




the moons reflection
breaks on the incoming waves -
end of a romance




the bagpiper
plays another tune-
shrieking children

standing on one leg
at the edge of the loch-
summer haze


morning rain-
the tea in the cup
cold

## **Survival**

nothing left
but to cast lots
for survival

an old rusted fence
playing host
to Basho's crow

circling,circling
the ravens
of tomorrow

waiting,waiting
to eat their fill
from todays drama

and as for us
we sit and wait
taking bites

out of each others
memories
regurgitating the past

heavy hail -
I pick up the pieces
of your smashed picture


throwing stones
into the lake-
the coldness of your words
the meaning
I tried to ignore
becoming crystal clear


summer drizzle -
the lonely call
of a young greenfinch

pounding rain -
a yellowhammer
heads for the hedgerow


picking flowers-
the decisions
that can't be changed


following
the suns shadow-
a garden snail

## **Wedding Day**

wedding photos-
a painted lady
on the brides bouquet

wedding disco-
the groom tries not
to pull a muscle

wedding night-
a moving cloud
reveals the moon

white satin-
the moonlight
through the window

after last nights rain
blue skies -
first day married

after
the honeymoon-
washing dishes

evening rain -
the chitter chatter
of goldfinches


reading
the latest obituaries -
autumn leaves


expecting a baby -
the poppy drops
its last petal


sound of rain
falling on the leaves
a greenfinches song

a sudden gust
sending the leaves twirling -
children playing tag



mid way
through an argument -
the space between waves



**Fragments**

and so
it all ended
the promises broken
and from the kitchen floor she sweeps
fragments

## **Hindsight**

evening
and a cool breeze
ripples the young barley
I never thought this would happen
to us



## **Tan-renga with Basho**

Awake at night -
the sound of the water jar
cracking in the cold
    listening intently
    the sound of my heart

## Early Summer

Morning heat -
sparrows sing
from the undergrowth

hiding
from responsibility
a quick diversion

taking the wrong path
the poppies
look just as radiant

setting goals
will this feeble flesh
ever reach achievement

drained from trying
a baby bird
sips from the fountain

all my enthusiasm
swallowed up
by my own imperfection

Juniper bonsai -
how many hands
have tended
your foliage
brought you to beauty ?


**Instability**

Morning
warmth of the sun
after the thunderstorm
my resolve starts to slip away
once more



Weather worn stone
still standing
after one thousand years
how many prayers were said ?
how many were answered ?

summer evening -
at the end of my street
a full moon

## Next Batsman

taking the field
the bowler looks at
the waving flag

polishing the ball
seeing red
at the umpires decision

hit for six
the fielder
adjusts his cap

slow ball
a flock of birds
flies overhead

out first ball
the long walk back
to the pavilion

ninety nine not out
the long silence
of the next ball

### Tan-renga with Buson
The spring sea:
all day long
undulating, undulating
    pacing back and forth
    with a colicy baby


### Tan-renga with Buson
white dew
a single drop
on each thorn
    quenching our thirst
    we re-tell old stories


### Tan-renga with Basho
Along this road
no one walks;
autumn evening
    after all this time
    still travelling as strangers

accumulating snow -
I move one more rejection
to the recycle bin


seismic testing -
a pilot whale
loses its way


chilly evening-
a circus poster
flaps in the wind


cloud burst-
all my data
disappears

returning
by a different path -
snowdrops




reaching for my tea -
the creak
of old leather




feeling old -
moss
on the bird bath




pink carnations -
the smell
of your absence

re-birth -
the garden buddha
painted blue


traffic jam -
a line of crows
on the telephone wire


morning
after the argument -
frost on the grass


between
winter and spring -
frost on the snowdrops

lost love -
the candle flame
flickers




snowdrops -
a winter of
goodbyes




misty moon -
a tawny owl
disturbs the night




on the forest floor
beneath the fallen oak -
seedlings

above the pines
the moon rises -
winter sunset


winters night -
a crescent moon
with empty arms


climbing roses -
lovers meet
close to midnight


in the park
two old friends meet for lunch -
bookends

Winter breeze -
from the pine branches
an owl's cry


Spring day -
a young hawk
catches the wind


light snow -
from the holly bush
a robins song


Snow sprinkled heather -
breaking the silence
a wrens song

end of a romance -
she hands the book
to the librarian


misty moon-
do you also see it
through tears?


freezing night -
homelessness
on the city streets


new year-
last years rain
still in my shoe

Winter rain-
the full moon
from leaf to leaf


Cold December day -
the wind speaks
of happier times


fallen oak tree -
a young robin
peeps through a hole


After the rainstorm -
the lightness
of birdsong

in the fading light
of a December day-
birdsong


tree shadows
across my path -
the solitude of winter


winter moon-
the silver birch
is re-born


morning worship -
songs of praise
from trees

morning rain -
the telephone wires
empty


singing
as we walk along-
skylarks


wandering
along a lonely road -
a strangers shadow


lonely walk-
watching my breath ascend
to the heavenly twins

city street -
even cherry blossom
goes unnoticed


Spring rain -
every field owns a different
shade of green.


the bare branches
of the cherry tree -
a cold North wind

between the clouds
Orion's belt-
windy night



Spring rain -
the sky still empty
of swallows



incoming tide -
plovers race ahead
of the waves

sunshine and showers -
this life
and all it holds



Spring day -
a crocus
salutes the sun



on the branch
of the giant redwood -
a butterfly

late February -
Brent geese gather
on the salt marsh




snow flurries -
a sparrow
withdraws into itself




raising my collar
against an icy wind -
a high moon

last autumns leaves
still astir -
the spring wind



along the fence rail
a blackbird chases a sparrow -
spring wind



bending
under the weight of winter -
an old tin shed

now the wind has gone
birdsong returns
to the empty space



an arrow in flight -
all the promises
you said you'd keep



all the things
that get in the way -
the sundials shadow

green tea -
against the window
a gentle rain



sea breeze -
something about you
in the evening tide



high tide -
water fills the empty space
of our feet

Printed in Great Britain
by Amazon